FEATURING

# JUNGKOOK

FACTS, QUIZZES, ACTIVITIES, AND MORE!

by Erin Falligant

CAPSTONE PRESS
a capstone imprint

Published by Capstone Press, an imprint of Capstone
1710 Roe Crest Drive, North Mankato, Minnesota 56003
capstonepub.com



Library of Congress Cataloging-in-Publication Data
Names: Falligant, Erin, author
Title: Featuring Jungkook : facts, quizzes, activities, and more / Erin Falligant.
Description: North Mankato, Minnesota : Capstone Press, 2026. | Series: Your favorite stars | Audience term: Children | Audience: Ages 8-11 | Audience: Grades 4-6 | Summary: "What are Jungkook's nicknames? What famous sporting event did he perform at? What challenges has he overcome? Jungkook's fans can learn the answers to these questions and others in this collection of fun facts, awesome photos, and more featuring the versatile star singer!"— Provided by publisher.
Identifiers: LCCN 2025023791 (print) | LCCN 2025023792 (ebook) | ISBN 9798875255120 (hardcover) | ISBN 9798875255076 (paperback) | ISBN 9798875255083 (PDF) | ISBN 9798875255090 (ePub) | ISBN 9798875255106 (Kindle edition)
Subjects: LCSH: Jungkook, 1997-—Juvenile literature | Singers—Korea (South)—Biography—Juvenile literature | LCGFT: Biographies
Classification: LCC ML3930.J85 F35 2026 (print) | LCC ML3930.J85 (ebook) | DDC 782.4216/3095195 [B]—dc23/eng/20250527
LC record available at https://lccn.loc.gov/2025023791
LC ebook record available at https://lccn.loc.gov/2025023792

Editorial Credits
Editor: Carrie Sheely; Designer: Elijah Blue; Media Researcher: Rebekah Hubstenberger; Production Specialist: Tori Abraham

Image Credits
Alamy: Collection Christophel, 47, Erik Pendzich, 39, Nancy Kaszerman/ZUMA Press Wire, 23 (top); Getty Images: Amy Sussman, 11, Arturo Holmes, 16, Dia Dipasupil, 31 (top right), Emma McIntyre, 36 (middle right), Frazer Harrison, cover, 25 (top), 32, Jamie McCarthy, 5, 14, 37, 43, Johnny Nunez, 45, Jon Kopaloff, 9, Kevin Dietsch, 24 (bottom), Kevin Winter, 35, 36 (middle left), Matt Winkelmeyer, 41, Michael Loccisano, 13 (top left), 19, Nina Westervelt/Variety, 17 (top), Rich Fury, 7, 29 (bottom right), 38, Rob Kim, 31 (left), Roy Rochlin, 21; Newscom: John Patrick Fletcher/Action Plu, 27; Shutterstock: A7880S, 23 (dog), Accogliente Design, 24 (chat icon), Agnwork (lightstick), cover, 29, Andrey Kozhekin, 17 (records), ANNA ZASIMOVA (rainbow chrome star), back cover and throughout, corund, 40, Daria Falcon, 42 (boots), Defona, 13 (middle right), derter (chrome sparkle), back cover and throughout, GraphixTreasure (character), cover, 9 , Haali, 44, Kate Zimneva (finger heart), cover, 12, Lana Brow, 45 (fashion men), Lidiia, 20, lilia_ahapova (3D hearts), 13, 29, Mashaart (silver star), back cover and throughout, mentalmind, 42 (sunglasses), MohammadKam, 42 (heart), MVshop, 42 (jacket), qaramelice, 10, Rinika25, 25 (heart headphones), Tuba Reza, 35 (heart chat icon), v_kulieva (blurry heart background), cover and throughout, Yuliia Sobolieva, 41 (glossy sparkle)



Printed and bound in China. 006461

# TABLE OF CONTENTS

CHAPTER 1

# THE FACE OF BTS

Born in Busan, South Korea, **JEON JUNGKOOK** was only 13 when he signed on with Big Hit Entertainment. By the age of 15, he was the lead vocalist of the South Korean boy band BTS. By age 25, he'd launched a solo career, and ***Rolling Stone*** magazine called him "one of the greatest singers of all time." So what makes Jungkook so special? That voice. He can hit the high notes, harmonize with his bandmates, and control his voice while dancing, which is difficult for many performers. That's a recipe for success!

## STAR SCOOP!

Jungkook has "perfect pitch," which is really rare—even for professional singers. That means if someone plays a note on the piano, Jungkook can name it without seeing which key was played!

# JUNGKOOK'S ROLES IN BTS

**THE MAIN VOCALIST, OR SINGER**—EVEN THOUGH HE'D NEVER HAD LESSONS!

**THE CENTER**, WHO STANDS IN FRONT FOR PERFORMANCES AND MOST PHOTO SHOOTS

**THE LEAD DANCER** ONSTAGE

**THE SUB-RAPPER**, WHO FILLS IN FOR OTHER RAPPERS WHEN THEY CAN'T PERFORM

**THE YOUNGEST BANDMATE**, CALLED THE GOLDEN MAKNAE (WHEN TRANSLATED FROM KOREAN TO ENGLISH THIS MEANS "GOLDEN YOUNGEST."

**THE FACE (AND MOST POPULAR MEMBER)** OF THE BAND

## STAR SCOOP!

Jungkook answers to many names. "Jung Kook" is his stage name, and his nicknames are "JK," "Jungkookie," and "Kookie."

# BAND OF BROTHERS

Jungkook has an older brother named Jeon Jung Hyun. But when Jungkook joined **BTS**, it felt like getting six more brothers: Suga, RM, Jimin, V, Jin, and J-Hope. He calls his bandmates *hyungs*, which means "older brothers" in Korean. "I watched them do music, their little gestures and the way they did their interviews, and I realized and learned things," he said. "SUGA's thoughts, RM's words, Jimin's actions, V's unique style, Jin's cheerfulness, J-Hope's optimism . . . Things like that all came into me one by one."

## STAR SCOOP!

The BTS song "Begin" is about Jungkook meeting his bandmates. Some of the lyrics translate to "A 15-year-old me with nothing. The world was so big and I was so small." Later lyrics say, "You make me begin. Smile with me."

V
SUGA
JIN
JUNGKOOK
RM
JIMIN
J-HOPE

## BTS TEST

How well do you know BTS? Decide which of these statements are true and which are false.

1. BTS stands for the Korean phrase *Banatan Sonyeondan*, which means "Boys Take a Stand."

2. Jungkook, J-Hope, and Jimin were called "3J" and did special performances together.

3. One of the nicknames for BTS is "Bangtan Boys."

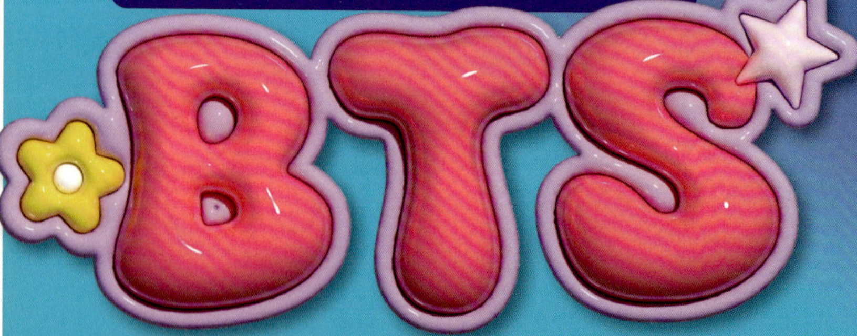

**4.** Two band members have perfect pitch.

**5.** All seven members had to serve in the South Korean military.

**6.** The band took a break in 2022.

**7.** Their first full-length album was called *Be*.

Answers: 1. False (It means "Bulletproof Boy Scouts."), 2. True, 3. True, 4. False (Only Jungkook has perfect pitch.), 5. True, 6. True, 7. False (It was called *Dark & Wild*.)

CHAPTER **2**

While most of Jungkook's bandmates were in the military, he pursued a solo music career. His first album, *Golden*, sold a record-breaking 2.1 million copies in just one day! The first single from the album, "Seven," shot to the top of the Billboard charts. It became the fastest song in history to reach 1 billion streams on Spotify. Jungkook was asked what the world could expect from him as a solo artist. His answer? "A whole new Jung Kook."

## STAR SCOOP!

The word "golden" has special meaning. When Jungkook's mom was pregnant with him, she had a dream about gold. After releasing ***Golden***, he said, "I feel that I'm shining the most right now. . . . I think now's my golden era."

# AN ACTION-PACKED YEAR

In 2023, Jungkook launched his solo career. He accomplished a lot!

**MUSIC VIDEOS RELEASED: 4**

**SHOWS PERFORMED IN: 10+**

**COUNTRIES VISITED: 5**

**SONGS OR "TRACKS" RECORDED: 12**

**DAYS IT TOOK FOR "SEVEN" TO REACH 100 MILLION PLAYS ON SPOTIFY: 6**

## STAR SCOOP!

Jungkook thought of everything he had to do as a list of quests. "I just took it step-by-step," he said, "and then I suddenly realized, 'Wait, I'm already here? I'm almost done?'"

# PARTNERING UP

Jungkook enjoys working with other musicians. Without his bandmates by his side, he partnered with famous singers including Charlie Puth and Usher. Jungkook invited rapper Latto to join him on the song "Seven." He featured rapper Jack Harlow on the song "3D" and later remixed the same song with Justin Timberlake. And the song "Too Much"? Jungkook cowrote that one with rappers The Kid LAROI and Central Cee, along with a few other writers including Justin Bieber!

Jack Harlow

Jungkook performing "Seven" with Latto in 2023

## STAR SCOOP!

Jungkook's favorite song on the album *Golden* was "Hate You," which was written with help from Canadian singer-songwriter Shawn Mendes.

# WHAT PEOPLE SAY ABOUT JK

Jungkook has been called . . .

"a perfectionist"
**—Son Sungdeuk, performance director**

"a musical prodigy"
**—*Music Grotto***

"a chameleon [who can] mold into any different kind of song"
**—Cirkut, producer**

"an extremely gifted singer"
**—*Rolling Stone* magazine**

"a genius that puts in the work"
**—Son Sungdeuk, performance director**

"the embodiment of pop music"
**—Pdogg, producer**

## STAR SCOOP!

Jungkook doesn't think of himself as a genius. He says, "I was just born a fast learner, and I think I use that to my advantage. . . . I look for ways to maximize what I've got."

CHAPTER 3

# FAN FOLLOWING

Jungkook is so grateful for the support of his fans that he has the word "ARMY" tattooed on his knuckles. That stands for Adorable Representative MC for Youth, the official name of BTS fans. After going solo, Jungkook's fans were called "Jungkookies" or "Kookies." But whatever you call them, Jungkook is as loyal to his fans as they are to him! He takes time to greet fans and chat with them using livestreams. Jungkook once said, "The best moment of my life is seeing ARMY from the stage, and that will never change."

A fan holds up a Jungkook figure at a performance in New York City.

## STAR SCOOP!

Jungkook has even written songs for his fans. He wrote the BTS song "Magic Shop" for ARMY as well as the solo songs "Still With You" and "My You."

# SOCIAL MEDIA SUPERSTAR

MOST SEARCHED K-POP IDOL ON PINTEREST IN 2024

MOST VIEWED INSTAGRAM REEL IN 24 HOURS BY A MALE ARTIST

SECOND MOST SEARCHED K-POP IDOL ON GOOGLE IN 2024

TOP K-POP STAR ON TUMBLR FIVE YEARS IN A ROW

MOST SEARCHED K-POP IDOL ACROSS ALL SOCIAL MEDIA PLATFORMS IN 2022

MOST TWEETS INCLUDED IN THE TOP MOST-LIKED LIST ON X

MOST VIEWED INDIVIDUAL LIVESTREAM ON WEVERSE IN 2024 (WITH 20.2 MILLION REAL-TIME VIEWERS IN ONLY THREE HOURS)

MOST VIEWED HASHTAG ON TIKTOK OF ANY SOLO ARTIST IN HISTORY, WITH BILLIONS OF VIEWS

MOST SEARCHED IDOL ON YOUTUBE FIVE YEARS IN A ROW

## STAR SCOOP!

Jungkook's Doberman, Bam, has his own Instagram account! He gained 1 million followers in only 14 hours and now has more than 7 million.

# THE JUNGKOOK EFFECT

Jungkook knows how to use his popularity for good. If his fans see him wearing something, they rush to buy it. So he rallies his ARMY to support causes he cares about. When he encouraged fans to buy from small businesses instead of bigger stores and chains, they did! "I was so grateful for the fans for making this happen," he said. What other causes does he care about? Supporting children's hospitals, animals in need, the environment, education, and disaster relief. If Jungkook cares about something, chances are good that his fans will too.

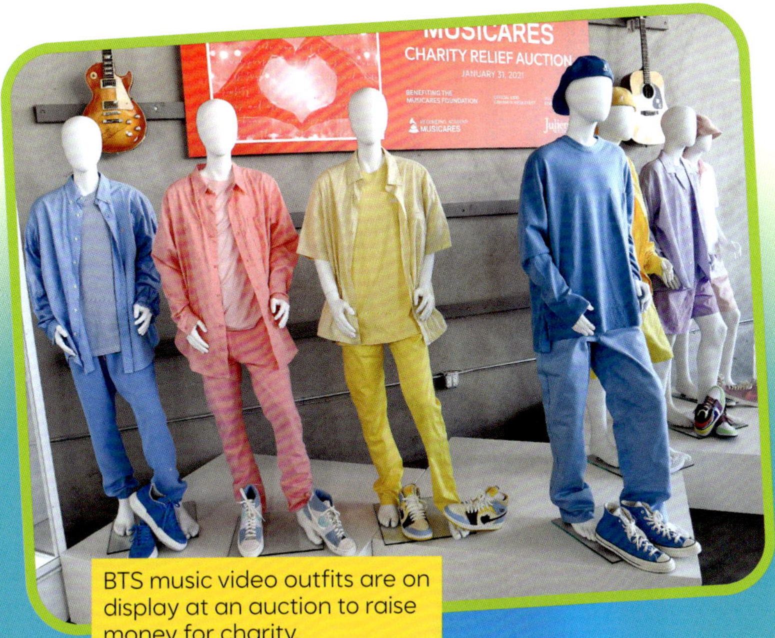


BTS music video outfits are on display at an auction to raise money for charity.

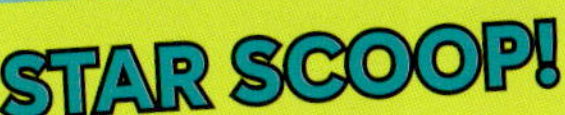

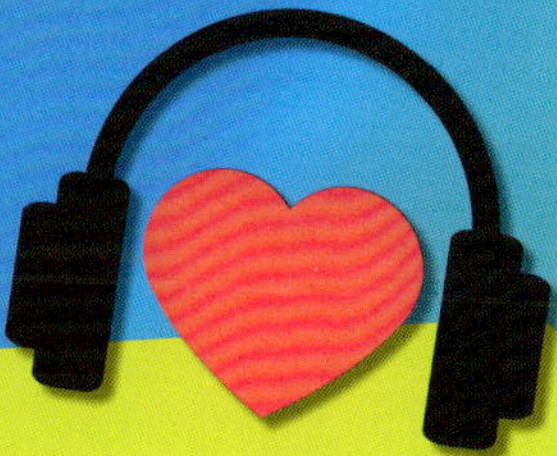

## STAR SCOOP!

During the COVID pandemic, Jungkook called on ARMY for help. They donated 2 billion Korean dollars to put toward education and healthcare.

CHAPTER **4**

# SONGS AND LYRICS

Jungkook was the first Korean solo artist to have seven songs hit *Billboard*'s Hot 100 list.

**"NEVER LET GO" —DEBUTED AT NUMBER 97**

**"STAY ALIVE" —DEBUTED AT NUMBER 95**

**"TOO MUCH" — FEATURING THE KID LAROI AND CENTRAL CEE— DEBUTED AT NUMBER 44**

**"LEFT AND RIGHT" WITH CHARLIE PUTH—DEBUTED AT NUMBER 22**

**"3D" FEATURING JACK HARLOW—DEBUTED AT NUMBER FIVE**

**"STANDING NEXT TO YOU"—DEBUTED AT NUMBER FIVE**

**"SEVEN" FEATURING LATTO— DEBUTED AT NUMBER ONE**

Jungkook performing for the World Cup in 2022

## STAR SCOOP!

Jungkook made history with his song "Dreamers." He became the first Asian artist to release a song for the World Cup. It was on the official soundtrack for the famous soccer competition.

## GUESS THE LYRICS

How well do you know Jungkook's song lyrics? Find out!

**1.** Monday, Tuesday, Wednesday, Thursday, Friday . . .

A. Five days of the week
B. Seven days a week
C. Each day of the week

**2.** When it's deep like DNA . . .

A. Something they can't take away
B. Don't you know I have to stay
C. You know it's sweeter than the rain

**3.** "So if you're ready, and if you'll let me . . .

A. I wanna start a commotion
B. Gonna give you a promotion
C. I wanna see it in motion

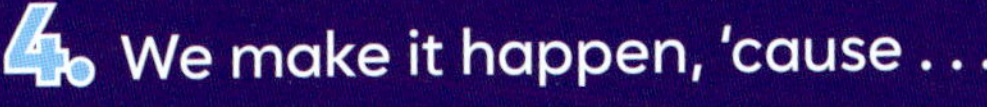

**4.** We make it happen, 'cause . . .

**A. We believe it**
**B. We can see it**
**C. Both A and B**

**5.** And when the days get longer . . .

**A. You fill my world with wonder**
**B. You help me feed my hunger**
**C. You make me see the wonder**

Answers: 1. B ("Seven"), 2. A ("Standing Next to You"), 3. C ("3D"), 4. C ("Dreamers"), 5. A ("Never Let Go")

# TWO LANGUAGES

With BTS, Jungkook sang mostly in Korean. But for his solo album ***Golden***, he recorded all his songs in English. He wanted to challenge himself and reach more fans around the globe. That wasn't an easy switch. Interviews used to be especially hard. "My English isn't good and so it was difficult to understand the conversations," Jungkook said. But he's been taking lessons and improving. And his fans love his songs, no matter what language they're in.

## STAR SCOOP!

Jungkook used to rely on his bandmate RM to do most of the talking during interviews. RM said he learned English partly by watching the TV show ***Friends***!

RM
citi
accenture
TimesLIVE

## DRAW JK-INSPIRED DOODLES

Jungkook enjoys creating artwork, including doodles. You can create artwork too. As a fun twist, make it JK-inspired! Find a sketch pad, and draw some of these:

- a sketch of a pet you love (maybe a Doberman, like Jungkook's?)
- a temporary tattoo you think a friend would like
- doodles you think would look good on a pair of canvas sneakers
- cover art for a Jungkook song or record
- something golden
- something inspired by Jungkook's lyrics

### STAR SCOOP!

Jungkook expresses himself through art as well as words. He has drawn doodles on J-Hope's shoes, a pencil sketch of Jin's dog, and tattoos for Jimin.

CHAPTER **5**

# BIG MOMENTS

Jungkook wows the crowd onstage, from his dance moves to how he connects with fans. He makes it look easy, but he puts in the work. "For every concert, Jungkook was always the last to leave rehearsals," said BTS performance director Son Sungdeuk. "When we were done and preparing to go home, we'd ask the members if any of them wanted to practice something more before calling it a day. Without fail, Jungkook would have his hand up." All that work has paid off. No one steals the spotlight quite like JK!

## STAR SCOOP!

Jungkook gets really nervous before performing. He once said, "When I sing live, my body will be in fear mode even if I don't want it to be." Who knew?

# MEMORABLE MOMENTS ONSTAGE

November 2021—performed with BTS at the American Music Awards and became the first Asian group to win Artist of the Year

2021

2022

April 2022—performed with BTS in what *Rolling Stone* called one of the greatest Grammy performances of all time; Jungkook entered the stage suspended from the ceiling!

November 2022—became the first Korean artist to perform at the World Cup.

July 2023—made his solo debut at the *Good Morning America* Summer Concert Series

## 2023

September 2023—became the first K-pop solo artist to headline the Global Citizen Festival

November 2023—surprised fans with a performance in New York City's Times Square

November 2023—taught Jimmy Fallon some dance moves on *The Tonight Show*

November 2023—performed his first full solo concert, *Golden: Live on Stage*

### STAR SCOOP!

Usher invited Jungkook to perform at the 2024 Super Bowl half-time show, but Jungkook had to say no. He was serving in the South Korean military at the time.

# PERFORMING UNDER PRESSURE

Before the 2022 **Grammy Awards**, Jungkook and J-Hope tested positive for COVID. They had only a day to practice with other bandmates before performing! A sore throat and a thunderstorm threatened Jungkook's first solo performance at the ***Good Morning America*** Concert Series in 2023, but Jungkook stayed positive. Afterward, he checked online to be sure his fans were happy. If he performs well, he often says it's "thanks to ARMY . . . ARMYs give me a confidence boost."

Jungkook performing at 2023 *Good Morning America* Concert Series

## STAR SCOOP!

Jungkook has said that even after good performances, "I think there must always be something I wish I'd done better. I think that's a given." He recognizes it and then moves on.

CHAPTER 6

# MANY TALENTS

Jungkook is known for his voice, but he's a skilled musician too. He plays piano, drums, and guitar. He's also an artist who loves to paint and draw. In fact, he created the SoundCloud cover art for a remix of the BTS song "Seesaw x I Need U." What else does Jungkook love? Sports, such as boxing and martial arts. He has a black belt in tae kwon do. If that weren't enough, he also enjoys directing and filming videos. He directed the music video for the BTS song "Life Goes On."

## STAR SCOOP!

As a young teen, Jungkook wasn't sure he even wanted to be a singer. He thought he might be an athlete or an artist instead.

# A PASSION FOR FASHION

Jungkook has inspired a lot of fashion trends. See how his style has changed over time.

## STAR SCOOP!

JK is called the "Sold Out King" because items he is photographed with sell out right away. This includes everything from the lip balm he uses to the clothes and shoes he wears.

## DESIGN A JK-INSPIRED OUTFIT

Trace the outline of a person onto a sheet of paper, and then design a Jungkook-worthy outfit.

- Go full-on emo black or Barbie pink.
- Add a plaid overshirt.
- Add accessories! Jungkook wears necklaces, earrings, hats, and beanies.
- Draw laces on his chunky boots.
- Doodle a graphic design on a T-shirt.

# ON-SCREEN SUCCESS

Jungkook has some TV and documentary credits to his name. He costarred with BTS bandmates in the South Korean reality series ***In the Soop***, which showed the seven K-pop stars spending time in nature. And before Jungkook and bandmate Jimin joined the military, they took a trip to Japan together. They filmed the trip and turned it into a travel reality series. Jungkook also stars in a film documentary called ***I Am Still***, which follows the first eight months of his solo career. Whether he's onstage or on-screen, Jungkook shines bright!

## STAR SCOOP!

Music is still JK's top priority. "There are still so many genres and styles of music that I have yet to try," he said. "So I want to continue singing, dancing, and performing onstage."

JUNG KOOK
I AM STILL
SÉANCES EXCLUSIVES AU CINÉMA
LES 21 ET 22 SEPTEMBRE
RÉSERVATIONS
JUNGKOOK-IAMSTILL.COM

# ABOUT THE AUTHOR

Erin Falligant has written more than 50 books for children. Her Joss series for American Girl, written about a young surfer with hearing loss, earned a 2020 Moonbeam Gold Medal Award. Erin draws from her master's degree in child clinical psychology to write advice books on changing bodies, standing up to bullies, making friends, and mastering mindfulness. To learn more about Erin and her books, visit www.erinfalligant.com.

**READ MORE ABOUT YOUR FAVORITE STARS!**

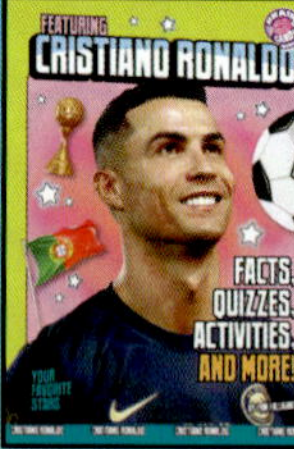

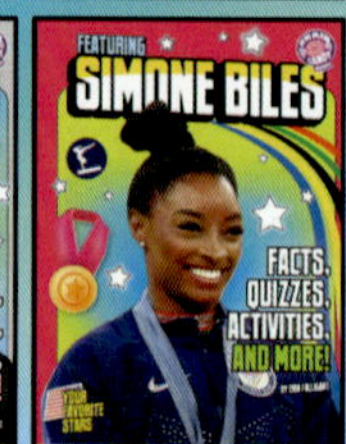